This Starfish Bay book belongs to

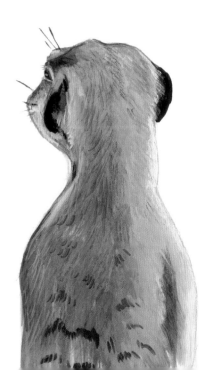

Whose Nose Do You Suppose?

Written by Richard Turner
Illustrated by Margaret Tolland

Whose nose do you suppose?

Meerkat

In faraway Africa, you will find this nose
where it's dusty and dry and not much grows.
A mammal with strong claws and marvelous eyesight
that sleeps in burrows to escape the cold desert night
in the morning stands tall to warm its belly in the sun,
and if it spies a predator, it's very quick to run.

Whose nose do you suppose?

Tiger

In Asia, this nose belongs to
the largest of cats,
with long, white whiskers,
as a matter of fact.
They can swim, they can run
and leap like no other,
and when they hunt,
it's under the cover
of dark, so you won't
see their stripes
prowling around deep
into the night.

Whose nose do you suppose?

Rabbit

This wriggling nose is found in almost every place.
Their teeth never stop growing. Where do they find the space?
They eat all manner of plants and even their own poop.
They live in burrows, some nests, some in a coop.
To some, they're a pet, to others a pest,
but one thing's for sure: their floppy ears are the best.

Whose nose do you suppose?

Elephant

In Africa and Asia, this nose is extra long.
The creature that owns it is incredibly strong.
This one is part nose and also part lip.
It can even do all manner of tricks.
It can breathe, it can grasp, drink, smell, and make sounds,
the most amazing animal nose going around.

Whose nose do you suppose?

Panda

This nose can be found lazing
in the mountains of China.
A creature that's large yet quite a good climber,
they don't reach for meat or even for fruit.
They prefer to dine out in their
black and white suit,
spending their time munching away
on juicy bamboo for most of the day.

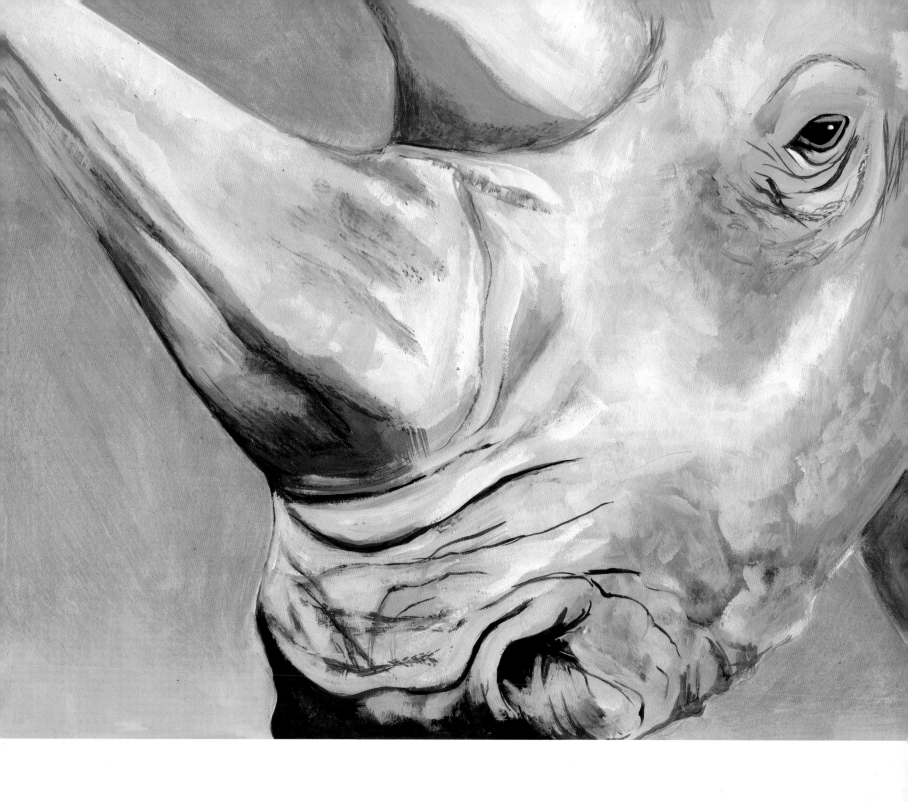

Whose nose do you suppose?

Rhinoceros

Nose-horn is the meaning of this mammal's name.
In Africa and Asia, you find its very large frame
eating day and night, so there's little time to play
only stopping to sleep in the heat of the day.
They enjoy lying in mud for a cooling soak
and oxpecker birds picking bugs off their coat.

Whose nose do you suppose?

Pink Flamingo

Though little sense of smell, it does have a beak,
a long, curved neck, and feathers so sleek.
With stilt-like legs and a rather pink color,
in the Americas and Africa, it stands out from all others,
especially when it's perched on only one leg,
which keeps its body warm, so it's said.

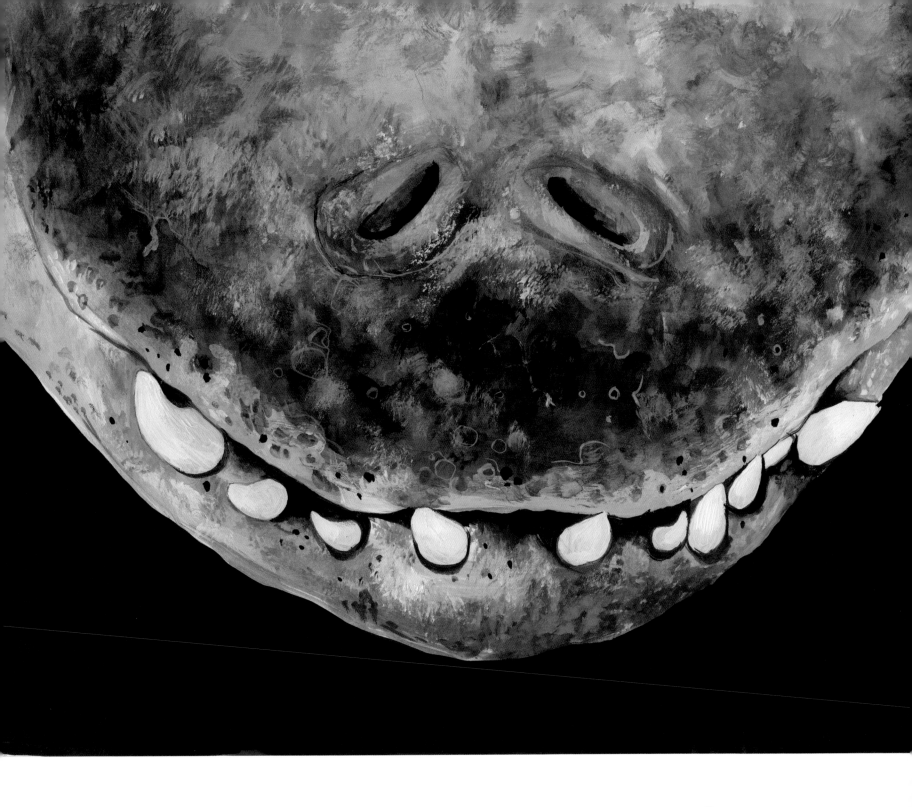

Whose nose do you suppose?

Alligator

This reptile has a wide, broad snout.
In America and China, it swims about
with gaping jaws and razor-sharp teeth,
it's one creature you don't want to meet.
If you see beady eyes floating by,
to stay well away would be wise.

Whose nose do you suppose?

Ostrich

From wildest Africa, this nose first came,
now found 'round the world, such is its fame.
With long neck and long legs, it is surely unique,
and two strong claws on two powerful feet,
a dangerous beak, and large eyes to spy.
It's a bird with wings, yet it cannot fly.

Whose nose do you suppose?

Great white shark

There's a fearsome jaw below this great nose
filled with very sharp teeth in seven scary rows.
One powerful tail and two dark piercing eyes,
they strike quick to take prey by surprise.
All 'round the world they swim with a grin.
Don't dare dive in if you see their fin.

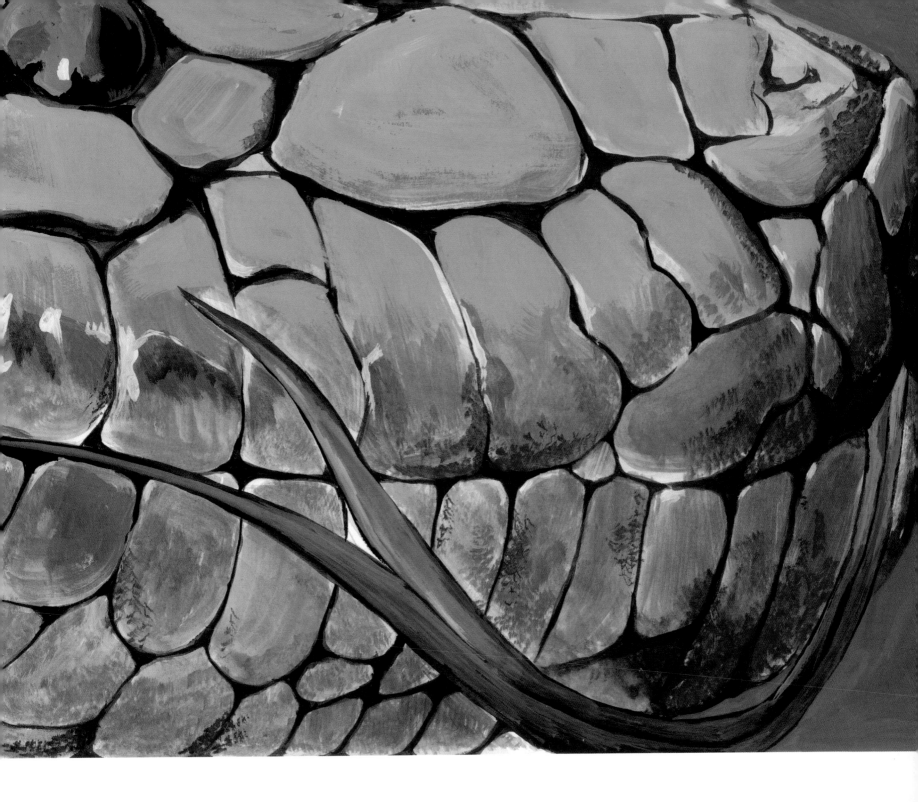

Whose nose do you suppose?

Anaconda

In South American waters,
this creature can be found,
in swamps and marshes
swimming around.
Eyes and nose above water and
body out of sight,
they sneak up on their prey
during the night
then squeeze and squeeze
in a very tight hold.
Jaws open wide then
swallow them whole.

Whose nose do you suppose?

Polar Bear

This nose doesn't look special,
but there's more to be told
of a creature that lives
where it's freezing cold.
Up in the Arctic is
where it can be found.
It can even out-smell the
nose of a bloodhound.
Its skin is black,
but its fur appears white.
When it slides on the ice,
it's quite a sight.

Starfish Bay® Children's Books
An imprint of Starfish Bay Publishing
www.starfishbaypublishing.com

WHOSE NOSE DO YOU SUPPOSE?

Text copyright © Richard Turner, 2019
Illustrations copyright © Margaret Tolland, 2019
ISBN 978-1-76036-062-7
First Published 2019
Printed in China by Toppan Leefung Printing Limited
20th Floor, 169 Electric Road, North Point, Hong Kong

Sincere thanks to Elyse Williams from Starfish Bay Children's Books for her creative efforts in preparing this edition for publication.

Richard Turner is a Performing Arts teacher, who supports children's creative voices through drama and dance. He has directed and choreographed musicals, working with students who can sing and dance way better than he can. Like most children, Richard has to be told to eat his peas, but never has to be told to eat his jellybeans or ice cream. He has been on a skateboard, a rollercoaster, an elephant and a camel. He has also been on a spaceship to the moon, but only in his dreams!

Margaret Tolland is an artist from New Zealand, whose illustrations are packed with detail. Through her work, get closer to the habitats and lifestyles of the many species, both flora and fauna, that she explores with an eye on environmental education. With twenty years' experience in visual arts education and working in a gallery, Margaret now illustrates full-time. Although she had a fear of spiders, after painting them in detail, she now appreciates how amazing they are.

For Mark Hanrahan,
A friend to one and all. –R.T.